Emotional Intelligence

A Guide to Improving Emotion Control and Understanding Relationships

By Lawrence Franz

I0427129

Introduction

What factors determine the success of an individual in their general life? Could it be powerful cognitive functions? Having a high IQ? There is no concrete answer for this question until you read through this book. In the early days, it was presumed that any individual who exhibited high levels of intelligence would automatically translate to a higher probability being successful. Parents, educators, and peers sang the same tune of high intelligence translating into greater success. We wish it was actually that simple!

If you have the desire of attaining success while living on this earth, you were required to study hard, score good grades, make it to the university, study harder, and graduate with an excellent degree/honors. This path was believed to be the guaranteed shot to a great job and an abundantly successful life.

You spent years believing this notion, and although it's not completely incorrect, it's not the full picture either. Success is the result of a combination of various factors, and the most fundamental of them is your ability to handle your own and other people's emotions.

Emotional intelligence, or emotional quotient, (both represent the same idea), is a type of intelligence that refers to an individual's ability to recognize and manage or control their own and other people's emotions. It is a simple and straightforward concept that comprises two main components:

- Identifying or recognizing emotions, intentions, desires, and goals in yourself and other people.

- Managing these emotions and actions to accomplish the most positive outcome for everyone involved.

Research on emotional intelligence has been ongoing since the mid-20th century within the psycho-scientific community. However, it wasn't until 1995, when Daniel Goleman published his book by the same name, that emotional intelligence rolled into the mainstream consciousness and became a groundbreaking concept. Back then, intelligence quotient (IQ) was seen as the only factor that mattered when it came to assessing an individual's capabilities. Once emotional intelligence took over, IQ was perceived as a narrow or limited way of assessing an individual's chances of success. The cutthroat world of career, jobs, and business was starkly different from the cushy confines of a classroom.

If one had to navigate the real world, they'd have to adapt to a different kind of intelligence than the academic one used in classrooms or libraries. A person's knowledge and cognitive abilities alone didn't guarantee success in life. A degree didn't automatically mean a high paying job or a profitable business.

At best, you'll get your foot through the door. However, for someone to succeed, you would need much more than just plain intelligence. It would take social, communication, conversation, and emotional skills to raise the bar. These are life skills that aren't taught in the classroom but are learned by living in a hostel, waiting at bars, joining social clubs, being a part of sports teams, and volunteering.

Make a list of ten successful people you admire the most. They are the people you look up to as they lead successful and balanced lives. Are all these folks top honors graduates from distinguished educational institutions with a high IQ? My money is on "No!"

Again, do not let yourself to misunderstand my goal at this point. I am not undermining the importance of intelligence or asking you to shut that book on mechanical engineering and start reading about human psychology. It is awesome if you possess naturally high cognitive abilities and a high intelligence quotient. All I am saying is, you should ideally have both EQ and IQ complementing each other to increase your chances of success in the real world. If you can increase your emotional quotient to back up an already high intelligence quotient, you can achieve many great things!

The objective of this book is to discuss crucial aspects of emotional intelligence and how to use them in your everyday life to make your dream of being successful a reality. We'll take a look at practical techniques to raise your emotional quotient and eventually boost your chances of success.

Chapter 1: Understanding Emotional Intelligence and Models

What is the essence of emotional intelligence? Having the ability to realize your emotions and those of other people who are around you and managing the emotions to get a wonderful and positive outcome.

Essentially, emotional intelligence (EQ) is the knack of perceiving, managing, and evaluating emotions to create the desired positive outcome. John Mayer and Peter Salavoy were the pioneers of emotional intelligence. The term was made popular by Daniel Goleman in 1995 with his groundbreaking book of the same name, *Emotional Intelligence*. However, emotional intelligence as a term was first used by Michael Beldoch in the mid-20th century.

It gives one the capabilities of controlling their feelings and those of others, differentiating emotions in various situations, and controlling the emotional information to drive your actions and what you think. This is a broader and more general definition of emotional intelligence, although there are differences within the scientific community about what it encompasses. The unanimous view is that it is a skill that involves identifying, understanding, and managing emotions.

Emotional Intelligence Ability Model

The emotional intelligence model was created by Mayer and Salovey, who defined emotional quotient as the ability to correctly recognize, evaluate, and generate emotions to facilitate thought, gain a better understanding of emotions, and manage emotions for enhancing both cognitive and emotional development.

The psychologist duo believed that an individual must be assessed on four distinct interconnected abilities to determine their overall EQ. The four abilities are:

Recognizing emotions

This involves picking up verbal and nonverbal clues for understanding a person's emotions.

Reasoning or using these emotions to facilitate thinking and intellectual activity

For example, leveraging emotions to offer solutions or reviewing situations. This helps us focus our limited attention span on the right things and react as per the situation. This benefits the overall creative process.

Understanding emotions

Human emotions are complex. They hold multiple meanings and guide us in understanding another person's emotional state of mind. Emotions give us a chance to understand other people and the emotions they are experiencing. Emotions are full of nuances and cannot be understood from a direct approach. Every emotion holds its own pattern of thoughts, actions, and intentions.

For instance, when an individual undergoes hurtful moments, you may be in a position to determine the reason for the hurting moments. An individual with this particular ability can immediately understand another person's emotional state and why they are thinking or behaving in a certain manner.

Regulating emotions

It involves the capacity of responding to emotions (both yours and those of other individuals) and handling them appropriately. For example, having the ability to contain the situation when another individual is upset or shows emotions of anger. Controlling our own and other people's emotions is a major component of emotional intelligence.

Salovey-Mayer concluded that an individual may be closed to emotional signals that are too painful or uncomfortable while being open to those that aren't overwhelming. This is calculated through the Mayer-Salovey-Caruso Emotional Intelligence Test (MESCEIT). It is measured by emotion-focused problem-solving.

Mixed Model Emotional Intelligence

This model of emotional intelligence was founded on Daniel Goleman's 25 distinct emotional intelligence traits, which encompasses everything from teamwork, service orientation, and accomplishment motivation to self-awareness.

The name mixed model is appropriate since it merges several traits of emotional intelligence with other personality characteristics that are not connected to intelligence and emotion. Emotional competence is a capability that can be learned and developed to create outstanding results. This emotional intelligence model is based on five primary categories, each one with clear emotional competencies:

- **Self-awareness**

Self-awareness is the ability to identify an emotion as we experience it. We tune in to our inner selves for assessing what exactly we are feeling and how to best regulate it. Self-awareness comprises self-confidence in your capabilities and emotional awareness in realizing what you are feeling and the subsequent emotional effects.

People with high self-awareness possess the following competencies:

They know the emotions they are experiencing and why they are experiencing these emotions.

They recognize how their emotions impact their performance.

They know their weaknesses and strengths.

Self-aware people are open to constructive criticism or feedback, fresher perspectives, constant learning, and personal development.

They are decisive by nature and can make clear decisions even when they're under stress and faced with uncertainties.

People with high self-awareness are able to establish the connection between people's feelings, thoughts, and actions.

They are able to display a sense of humor and view themselves from a lighter perspective. People who indulge in self-deprecating humor are often confident, self-assured, and emotionally intelligent people.

People with high self-awareness do not feel the need to go with the tide. They are happy to stand alone and voice views that do not match popular views.

- **Self-regulation**

Self-regulation is the ability to manage disturbing emotions and emotional impulses that can hinder interpersonal relationships and performance. We think we don't have great control over our emotions, but negative emotions can be managed through various self-regulating techniques like walking, prayer, running, and meditation. To self-regulate effectively, one needs to have control over their impulsive actions, must demonstrate honesty and integrity, possess creative thinking, must be able to handle change easily, and can take responsibility for their actions.

Here are some competencies that people with high self-regulation possess:

People with high emotional self-control can manage their impulses and disturbing emotions effectively.

They are able to stay calm, positive, and unaffected even in the most trying circumstances.

People with high self-regulation are able to build trust and credibility through reliability, integrity, and authenticity. They are also able to accept their own mistakes and are brave enough to call out others for their unethical acts.

High self-regulation abilities lead these people to meet commitments, keep promises, and act on their word.

They are also highly effective in handling change and adapting to new scenarios.

Motivation

Motivation is the ability to work toward fulfilling a set of goals. The most important aspect of this category is positive thinking. To become a positive thinker, one must always stay positive and be capable of restructuring negative thoughts. This can be accomplished by optimism, commitment, initiative, and drive for achievement. You are perpetually involved in the pursuit of improving yourself to become a better person.

Empathy

Empathy is the ability to not just discern people's emotions but also to "feel" what they feel. Empathy is about understanding others, being able to anticipate other people's needs, helping others develop their qualities, and building relationships with people who are quite different from you. Empathy is comprised of more than a single ability. However, fundamentally, it is about being able to feel and relate to other people's emotions.

People who have high empathy possess the following abilities:

They are extremely perceptive to verbal and nonverbal emotional clues while listening to people.

They show understanding for another person's point of view even though they may not necessarily agree with it.

They are happy to help solve people's problems and concerns in any manner within their capacity.

People with high social awareness acknowledge other people's accomplishments and reward them for their strengths.

Social skills

Relating to other people is another important attribute of emotional intelligence. Social skills are important in teamwork, collaboration, communication, influence, building relationships, and conflict management.

People with high social skills possess the following competencies:

They are able to deal with conflicts in an assertive and straightforward manner.

They embrace open communication and are ready to accept both compliments and criticism.

People with high social skills can inspire others to pursue a shared goal or vision.

Impact of Emotional Intelligence – Examples

Let us say you've been offered constructive feedback by your manager about areas you can improve upon or areas where you didn't perform to your fullest potential. People with a low emotional quotient may take the criticism personally or come up with a host of excuses and blame games to cover their shortcomings. They may not accept their mistakes or they may find a scapegoat to blame their inefficacy on. They may get angry, irritable, depressed, and demotivated. Acting on emotions is easier. Identifying them and regulating them takes work.

Conversely, an individual with greater emotional intelligence will accept the fact that no one is perfect. Rather than taking the feedback personally, they'll introspect about what their manager said and work on areas of improvement to become more efficient. They will stop making similar mistakes. People with a high emotional quotient will actively seek feedback from others rather than focus on proving themselves right. They are less likely to argue and blame others for their shortcomings.

Emotionally intelligent people are open to suggestions and constructive feedback, which eventually helps them accomplish their objectives. For these folks, being right is being more efficient. They value feedback and actively work on it. This is just one of the ways high emotional intelligence can positively affect your productivity and success in the workplace.

Let us now take another example in a personal scenario.

You are involved in a heated discussion about political ideologies with your best friend. While your friend is fervently putting forth their views about their ideology, you firmly stick to your opinion. When they speak, they appear angry. An emotionally intelligent person can quickly gauge this emotion and understand the impact of the topic on their friend. You realize that you could end up hurting or upsetting them if the topic continues for a while.

A person with high emotional intelligence gets a grip on the circumstances easily and gently acknowledges the other person's view even if they don't necessarily subscribe to those ideas. They may not agree with their friend, but they are accepting their right to disagree. Since this person is more thoughtful, empathetic, and sensitive to other people's needs, they can successfully stop a discussion from blowing into a full-fledged fight. Thus, things finish on a constructive and positive note.

Now, consider the same scenario with a person who isn't emotionally intelligent or empathetic toward other people's feelings. This kind of person is adamantly focused on their views. They refuse to understand where the other person is coming from. Thus, the discussion snowballs into a heated argument. They fan the flame of the difference even more. The results are anger, hurt, and negativity. The fight ends badly and affects their interpersonal relationship.

We can all identify that one emotionally intelligent person within our family, friends, or social circle. They always pick the most appropriate thing to say in any situation. They can pacify people, thwart potentially uncomfortable situations, nip arguments in the bud, and arrive at a solution where everyone is pleased. Irrespective of how tricky a scenario is, they manage to find their way through it by using emotional information about their own and other people's feelings.

They excel in handling challenging situations that involve differences between people and know how to assert themselves without offending anyone. These are the empathetic, considerate, and caring folks who also know how to assert themselves. It's no wonder that most companies today demand people with high emotional intelligence for filling leadership positions.

While people with a high intelligence quotient may have the answer or solution to your problems, emotionally intelligent people can make you feel more hopeful about the situation.

Chapter 2: Learn the Difference between Intelligence Quotient and Emotional Quotient

A good intelligence quotient or IQ is helpful for life. Knowing and understanding how to make logical and rational decisions is advantageous to everyone. At the same time, that IQ can only take people so far.

For instance, Jeffrey, a business executive, has a very high IQ. He has thought of many useful ideas for his business, and yet he is unable to get his business to expand or grow. He is having a hard time maintaining his payroll because people are constantly leaving the business.

Why is Jeffrey unable to get his business to grow? He is struggling with his EQ. He is not fully appreciative of his employees. Perhaps he does not understand that they need some balance between their work and their personal lives. This includes issues where workers are not satisfied with their jobs or are feeling too tired or uncomfortable with their work. But Jeffrey does not have the empathy to understand this.

As a result, it becomes hard for even his smartest ideas to thrive and grow. If he had a better EQ, he would make more plans based on what other people need. By adapting his ideas and values around what others want, it would become easier for his business to grow and thrive.

It is through one's EQ that it becomes easier to evolve and change.

What Makes It Different from Personality?

What makes EQ different from a person's standard personality? EQ focuses more on feelings while the personality is all about a person's style.

There are three things that make up every person:

1. The intelligence quotient
2. The emotional intelligence
3. General personality

Personality is hard-wired into one's brain. It is how a person would interact with others and behave in some fashion. Someone's personality can never change.

EQ is different as a person can develop it over time. When a person is trained well, it becomes easier for that person to be active and positive. Many points about improving one's EQ will be covered throughout this guide to provide simple ideas for what they can do to get their lives to move forward.

A person's IQ is likely to stay the same throughout one's life. A person has a certain ability to learn things at a specific rate. It might be easier for a person to learn emotions and how to manage them if that person's IQ is not low.

EQ might be related to IQ when all is considered. When a person's EQ is high, it becomes easier for someone to want to learn. That person will use one's IQ to one's advantage. The emotions become balanced so that people fully understand what they can do to grow their lives. As a result, a person will use one's intelligence at a slightly better rate.

The emotional intelligence that a person holds is important for all people who want to accomplish the most in their workplaces.

Chapter 3: The Golden Benefits of Emotional Intelligence

Emotional intelligence is more than just something related to knowing what people feel. It is to understand and recognize what can be done to help others or to at least get along with them.

It is through a person's EQ that someone can get the most out of life. When the level of emotional intelligence of a person is high, their probability of success and enjoying improved work performances is high. There are several positives of one's EQ that must be explored. These points are vital for the workplace in particular as they relate to what people can do to move forward and thrive in their jobs.

Get Along with People

A workplace is often a challenging place. Each person brings their personalities, their biases, and their different levels of intelligence and experience to the work environment. They have to work in harmony and this is not always easy. There is also the added pressure of competition involved. Personal relationships outside of the workplace can also be difficult at times. People often struggle with maintaining friendships.

Finding a long-lasting romantic relationship can be challenging to some people.

Those with a high EQ are better equipped to get along with others. A high EQ individual is able to understand the ups and downs that face relationships. They are able come up with smart and clear strategies that will see such conflicts avoided and solving any disagreements amicably.

Become More Productive

With high emotional intelligence, the productivity of such individuals is seen to be of high standards. Those people understand what they want out of their lives and aren't afraid of putting in the effort.

On the other hand, people with a low emotionally intelligent or not at all are unable to take control of their thoughts making them to be less productive. A person might become overly worried when a new task is introduced and it is different from what one might be used to. A person with a low EQ might be afraid of what will happen if a project does not go right. All that worry and fear will cause a person to not do well with a task, thus falling into the trap of not knowing what to do to fix a problem or make things work right.

Stay Accountable

People often shift their responsibilities and try to keep things from being too complicated. They don't want to do things because they resist doing it, or maybe they are not aware of what to do to fix the problems that happen. Others might not be aware of the circumstances surrounding what they are doing.

Accountability is a necessity for people in any workplace. A person who is accountable for one's actions and work is not afraid to accept responsibility for their actions. Maturity of an individual is shown through accountability. It is the measure that provides them with insight of understanding the functions and duties they have to undertake on a daily basis. This includes not only what is done correctly but also any errors that might occur. A person with a strong EQ will be more likely to stay accountable.

Accountability provides a person with the ability to take control of a situation. That person will understand that they are doing something valuable or necessary. By working with the right plans, it becomes easy for a person to stay accountable and confident with what one is going to do with life.

Easier to Manage Risks

There are risks to everything in life. A person might get into a car and drive to the grocery store, but that someone is getting into the risk that the car will malfunction or someone might cause an accident on the road. Meanwhile, a person who plays gridiron football might enjoy playing it, but that individual has the risk of suffering a substantial injury like a concussion.

There are risks involved in every aspect of every workplace. One of the greatest reasons why errors are often made in the workplace is because workers are not fully aware of the risks and what they can do to lessen them. This can cause people to panic when something happens that they did not anticipate. They might not have the emotional fortitude to handle some of the events that occur. Those who can handle and figure out their emotions will have an easier time moving forward and keeping everything under control.

A person's emotional intelligence can be utilized to figure out what one's abilities are and how well certain tasks may be completed. Knowing what can be done to fix issues and having a plan for emergencies is essential.

Avoid Questions

When a person has a low emotional intelligence, they are not certain about the decisions they make. They lack self-confidence. One of the most common questions that a person might ask is what they were thinking about in the past? For instance, a man who made a difficult move in the past might ask himself, "What was I thinking? I can't believe I did something that way. Why did I do that?" That man would have failed to use his emotional intelligence. People make rash decisions when they are not thinking about the results or consequences. They might think about the results that they want to attain, but they never think about why they want it or what they can do to maintain those results.

Emotional intelligence is needed to help people to have faith in what they are deciding to do. People need emotional intelligence to stay comfortable and focused on whatever it is they want to work on. More importantly, there will be less confusion when a person's EQ is strong. That person will not question their own decisions. People with a high EQ will not likely ask questions of other people in the workplace or in other situations. A person who asks lots of questions is revealing their low self-esteem and low self-confidence.

A Matter of Trust

People are loyal to people who they trust. One person might seem to be more intelligent than another, but what if that smarter person is difficult for people to trust? That intelligent person might be seen as stubborn or difficult to work with. An intelligent person might not have the emotional intelligence needed to deal with people. When EQ is missing, that person is not capable of understanding or having empathy toward others. But when a person has a high emotional intelligence, that person becomes easier to trust. This leads to added success and control over any situation.

It is through trust that people can stay positive around others. When people trust each other, they are willing to support one another through anything that might come about in the workplace. Trust focuses on people showing that they recognize each other's emotions and are willing to support each other. People who trust one another are likely to get along and feel better in each other's company.

Without trust, it becomes hard for a business to grow and thrive. More importantly, a personal or romantic relationship will not get off the ground if the people involved do not trust each other.

Managing Customers

An interesting part of working with EQ is that it concentrates on how well people are able to interact with each other in a workplace. This includes working with customers in a smart manner.

It is easier for businesses to grow when its employees have EQ. An employee needs a high EQ to have a sense of empathy with customers. When a person understands the emotions of others it becomes easier for that someone to market a product. Having an understanding of emotions is vital for success. This is especially true of the workplace when customers are involved. Every customer should be treated with respect and care to ensure there are no problems that can't be dealt with.

Let's say that Cherry is working to sell a car. She might notice that a customer is nervous about the process of buying a car. She can empathize with the customer and talk with that person about the process. Cherry might explain what makes a car an attractive investment. She may also identify questions that people have and provide smart answers to those issues. By using her EQ, Cherry is getting in touch with the customer and is showing that she cares about that customer's needs. This will make it easier for her to sell the car to that customer.

It is through the EQs of its employees that relationships with customers can be built. When the employees are capable of working with customers well, it becomes easier for people to feel comfortable with each other while doing business.

Chapter 4: Simple Art of Boosting Your Emotional Self-Awareness

It is of great essence to build your self-awareness as way of achieving high emotional intelligence. This is a wonderful way of giving yourself the full comprehension of your emotions and feelings. You can regulate your emotions for an optimally positive outcome only if you are able to identify these emotions. Labeling emotions and determining your actions based on these emotions is critical to the process of developing emotional intelligence. When you are more aware of your feelings and emotions, recognizing other people's emotions becomes simpler.

Here are solid, proven tips for boosting self-awareness to get you started on the path of emotional intelligence:

Label Your Emotions

Label and categorize your emotions. I know this makes your feelings sound like they belong to a library. However, labeling, or giving names to your emotions, makes it easier to identify and act upon them. When you feel an emotion surging through you, attempt to identify it quickly. Is it fear, insecurity, jealousy, anger, elation, depression, surprise, or a combination of these emotions?

Identify the triggers that cause these emotions. For instance, a specific person may evoke jealousy in you because you feel they are more successful than you.

Why do you experience certain emotions? What are the triggers that anger or hurt you? What makes you happy and sad? What is the source of positive and destructive emotions in you? Labeling your feelings and recognizing the stimuli for various emotions will increase your emotional self-awareness.

Grab a pen and paper to list your emotions when you experience a compelling feeling. Mention the precise emotion or feeling that you are experiencing. Accompany this emotional label with the trigger that caused it. What is it that made you feel the way you do? When you recognize an emotion, it is easier to manage it.

For instance, let us assume you feel a deep sense of loathing for a person without any specific reason. You dislike them and can't stand them, but funnily, can't tell why you dislike them. Upon closer examination of your feelings, you realize you dislike them because you are envious of them. You may believe they are always having a wonderful life, while things never go your way. By nailing this emotion as jealousy, you can regulate your potentially negative emotions.

Once you recognize the emotion as irrational jealousy, you will view it in a more logical and understanding manner. You'll begin to think along the lines that it isn't really someone's fault that they lead an amazing life. In fact, they should be applauded for working hard toward their goals. You'll realize that no one has a perfect life. Everyone goes through shares of trials and tribulation to attain success, which isn't necessarily visible to the outside world. Sometimes, it is only how we perceive things and not the reality. Thus, once you are more mindful of your emotions, you can work with them more positively.

Be an Expert on Yourself

What is the one thing you should do to bring about changes in your thoughts, actions, and behavior? The answer is: awareness about these thoughts and subsequent actions! To make changes, you ought to know what you have to improve upon.

Knowing yourself inside out is the key to being more emotionally aware and savvy. Did you know athletes are trained to identify and overcome feelings before an important upcoming game? If you are able to identify and take full control of the emotions that you experience, your productivity won't be affected.

Go back and think about all the recent instances where you let emotions get the better of you and affect your productivity. Haven't you let trivial matters impact your performance?

By being aware of your strengths and weaknesses, it is easier to confidently accomplish your objectives. There is a lesser scope for frustration, low productivity, and disappointment. Self-confidence increases your assertiveness while you express your thoughts and opinions, which is important for developing social skills.

Once you gain greater awareness, you will rarely be ruled by emotions. You have a clear edge if you are able to regulate your emotions. An emotionally aware person stops being a victim of their emotions and uses these emotions in a positive way to reach a desired outcome.

Spend Time Recognizing Areas of Development to Strengthen Them

- List all your strengths and weaknesses.

- Take a formal, psychological personality assessment test that helps you discover your own skills, abilities, limitations, and values.

- Obtain objective feedback from people you trust.

One way that works wonders for increasing your self-awareness is journaling. Write in a flowing stream of consciousness about the thoughts you are feeling and experiencing as they are occurring. What are the emotions you are experiencing? How do you react to the feelings physiologically? Are you experiencing a faster heartbeat, sweaty palms, increased pulse, and so on?

Emotions aren't always straightforward. In fact, they are complex and multilayered. For example, you may have a heated argument with your partner and feel angry, hurt, upset, and vengeful all at the same time. Write emotions exactly as you are experiencing them, even if two emotions appear to contradict each other. For instance, if you've got a scholarship to study overseas, you may be elated at the opportunity. However, the thought of leaving behind your partner may cause a twinge of sadness, too. You are acknowledging and validating your emotions by writing them.

Make a list of every role you play in your daily life such as being a parent, sibling, volunteer, worker, and more. What are the emotions linked with each role? For example, you may enjoy your role as a parent, but you can also be an unhappy employee. Examine every role and the emotions attached to it carefully.

Naming emotions linked to every relationship will help you manage emotions within that relationship more efficiently. It will keep you in greater control of your emotional reaction where the specific role is concerned.

Do a Frequent Check-In

Do a frequent check-in with your emotions much like how you have a waiter checking in with you frequently to know if you need anything. You do a mental check-in of your emotions periodically to understand how you are feeling at different times during the day. It is a sort of, "Hello, mind, how are you feeling? What can be done to make you feel better?"

Examine where the specific feelings come from. Are you feeling low and deflated because your boss said something to you in the morning? Are you feeling angry and hurt because you fought with your partner? Are you experiencing certain physiological symptoms as a result of these emotions or feelings? Are these emotions impacting your body language, posture, gestures, and expressions? Are these emotions evident or visible to others? Are you more transparent when it comes to expressing your emotions? Are your decisions primarily determined by emotions?

If you want to be a more emotionally balanced person, reconnect with your primary emotions, recognize them, accept the emotions, and use them for making better decisions.

Use Third Person

Research in the field of labeling our emotions has indicated that when we distance ourselves from our emotions, or view them more objectively, we gain higher self-awareness. Next time you feel the urge to say, "I am disappointed," try to say, "Andrew is disappointed."

If that seems too preposterous, try saying, "I am presently experiencing sadness," or, "One of my feelings at the moment is sadness."

These are techniques through which you are distancing yourself from overpowering emotions to stay naturally composed. You are basically treating your emotions as just another piece of information rather than being overwhelmed by them.

Each time you find yourself experiencing an urge to react to a situation, take a moment to name it. Then use it in the third person to distance yourself from intense emotions.

Emotions Don't Always Need to be Fixed

You don't always have to identify emotions with the intention of fixing them. Self-awareness is not about fixing emotions. It is about recognizing these emotions and letting them pass rather than allowing them to get the better of you. Society has conditioned us to think that certain emotions are bad. We mistakenly believe that experiencing these emotions makes us a bad person.

Far from it, emotions aren't good or bad. They are just that, emotions. There's no need to push away the seemingly bad emotions. Acknowledge that you are experiencing an emotion by saying something like, "I am experiencing jealousy." Practice deep breathing for a while until the emotion passes. Rather than pushing the emotion away and, in the process, increasing its intensity to come back even stronger, gently acknowledge it and let it be until it passes.

It takes around six seconds for the body to absorb chemicals that can alter your emotions. Give your body that much time.

We often share a hostile relationship with our emotions. They are believed to be something that is negative and should be fought or suppressed. However, emotions are information that helps us function in our daily lives. Overcome the mindset that emotions are good or bad, and instead focus on using them to empower you. Rather than letting emotions take control of you, use emotional information to work with them.

Emotions are neural hormones that are released as a direct response to our perceptions regarding the world. They direct us toward a specific action. All emotions have a distinct message and objective, which means there's no such thing as a good or bad emotion.

For example, fear helps us focus on an impending danger and take the necessary action to defend ourselves. Similarly, sadness makes us experience a sense of loss and facilitates a better understanding of what we truly care about.

If you move away from your best friend and become sad, this means you truly care about them so much that you experienced sadness. This is valuable information. Hence, sadness is not a bad emotion. It can determine the things or people that mean a lot to you.

If you use emotions as information for recognizing feelings, they can be channeled positively. The number one rule for developing higher emotional intelligence is to stop judging and curbing your emotions.

Train Yourself to Identify Emotions Based on Physiological Reactions

Our emotions often have physical manifestations. For example, you may feel anxious before a job interview or an important presentation. You experience the sensation of having "butterflies in your stomach" before addressing an audience on the stage.

Don't you find your heart pounding with excitement when you are about to go on a date with someone you've fancied for long?

Nervousness leaves us with sweaty palms and stiff muscles.

While these are only some of the physiological reactions we experience with our emotions, research has proven that a variety of emotions are strongly associated with stimulating certain parts of the body.

Regular patterns of physical sensations are linked with each of the six fundamental emotions, including fear, happiness, anger, sadness, disgust, and surprise. Human emotions discreetly overlap physiological sensations. For example, lower limb sensations are associated with sadness. Similarly, increased upper limb sensations are connected with anger. A strong feeling of disgust generates sensations within the throat and digestive system. Fear and surprise generate sensations in the chest.

Identify Recurring Patterns

This can be one of the most effective parts of knowing yourself. Neuroscience will help you understand the process more effectively. Our brains have an inherent tendency to follow established neural paths rather than creating new ones. This doesn't necessarily mean that the established patterns are serving us positively or that they can't be altered.

For instance, when a person becomes angry, they may bottle up their emotion rather than express it. This has become an emotional pattern with the person and is deeply embedded in the mind. However, awareness of this pattern can help the person chart another course of action, where the person practices responding instead of simply reacting to the emotion. However, the first step to charting a new pattern is identifying a pattern.

Recognize the build-up of emotions before something suddenly triggers you. These triggers have a predictable pattern. If you are already frustrated, you are more likely to see a situation in a more negative light. Similarly, if you are overcome by fear, you are more likely to interpret a stimulus as a threat. Come up with a pattern that is predictable and be in the know of such biases and their effects towards your emotions. The more efficient you become in recognizing your biases, the lower your chances of misinterpreting a stimulus.

Work with What You Know about Emotions

Emotions are important pieces of data that help you gauge things from a clearer and objective perspective. Don't suppress, ignore, fight, or feel overwhelmed by your emotions. Instead, you should build a valuable library of experiences with them. The purpose of emotional awareness is to concentrate our attention on these emotions and use them positively to create the desired outcome.

Treat your emotions as data that relies on your view of the world, or as a guide on how to act. When you open yourself to this data, you enjoy access to a huge resource of emotions that can be utilized to drive your actions in the right direction. With a defined emotional route, you will find it easy to know where you have to move and reach as intended. Therefore, you should acknowledge and recognize your emotions as data, and work with them instead of trying to beat them.

Begin by carefully noticing how you feel at the moment. Observe emotions without judging them or attempting to fix them. Learn to simply notice your emotions.

Be open to Feedback and Constructive Criticism

If you wish to build a great awareness channel of your emotions, then you need to welcome any feedback and criticism emanating from other individuals. For instance, a friend may tell you that each time they talk about their accomplishments they sense your pangs of envy or dislike toward them. This may help you tune into your emotions and emotional triggers more effectively.

Emotionally intelligent folks are open to receiving feedback, and they always consider the other person's point of view. You may not necessarily agree with them, but listening to other people's criticism and feedback helps you work on your blind spots. This can help you recognize your thoughts, triggers, and behavioral patterns.

I know a person who, in a bid to increase his self-awareness and emotional quotient, actively goes around asking people for feedback about his words, feelings (as they understand it), and actions. It acts as an emotion meter, which helps him gain greater awareness of his emotions and regulate them more efficiently.

Chapter 5: Calmly Manage Your Stress

Stress decreases your ability to control your emotions. When you're stressed, you're more likely to feel anxious and depressed. You'll have mood swings.

Stress keeps you from tuning in to your negative emotions and from practicing any of the things we have discussed in this book.

When you are stressed and not in a position to manage it, it becomes hard to recognize the emotions at work; neither will you be able to think about them before acting on them. More so, you would acutely avoid your negative emotions. This prevents you from experiencing them and becoming conversant with them. Therefore, it is important that you carve out a method to manage stressful situations. The most important thing when you are stressed is to remember to be calm and to detach as much as possible, usually progressively, from the source of the stress. Sometimes, this could even be people.

Practice Mindfulness

Mindfulness is a very important tool for enhancing emotional intelligence. It is the ability to be emotionally present in the moment without judgment. To practice mindfulness, you must focus your attention on the emotions you are feeling and the signals they are sending into your environment including how they affect any interactions you might be having.

You must also not judge your emotions. Allow them to manifest. That is like saying "feel them." This is so that you can recognize them. Do not suppress them. Take notice of the emotional buildup of the person you are interacting with too before deciding whether or not to act on your own emotions.

Chapter 6: Solid Steps to Improve Interpersonal Connection

We've established in earlier chapters how emotional intelligence is the master key to effective leadership and social skills. By tuning into other people's emotions or by empathizing with how they feel, there is a higher chance that you will respond appropriately to create the desired positive result. Thus, our ability to connect with our own and other people's emotions can be a powerful tool in social and leadership situations.

Understanding other people, helping overcome stress situations, motivating your team, negotiating business deals, and building a close-knit social circle becomes easier when you can use the emotional information you have about them as leverage. It increases situational awareness and our ability to read people, thus helping us make the most positive decision.

Here are some verbal and nonverbal factors impacting social-emotional quotient, or our ability to read and deal with people:

Body Language

Research reveals that body language accounts for 50 percent of our communication. You'd wonder why there were words in the first place if body language accounts for half the communication process. Tuning in to a person's body language will help you pick up important signals related to their emotional state and subconscious thoughts or feelings.

Here's a quick cue sheet to reading people's feelings through their body language:

- Crossed arms and legs are signals of people creating a subconscious barrier. They are emotionally closed, suspicious, or do not subscribe to your ideas. They aren't open to listening to your views or are disinterested in the topic of conversation. You may have to emotionally open the person up a bit by changing the topic and then get back to the original topic. The physical act of uncrossing their arms and legs will make them more subconsciously receptive to your ideas.

- How can you tell a genuine smile from a fake one? Simple, it's all in the eyes. Observe that there's crinkled skin near the person's eyes forming crow's feet. People often present a happy expression to hide their true feelings. However, if their smile doesn't cause the skin around their eyes and mouth to crinkle, they are most likely not as happy as they are pretending to be. Artificial smiles create wrinkles only around the mouth, while genuine smiles create wrinkles around the sides of the eyes.

- When people constantly take their gaze away from you while speaking, they are most likely not being very honest or trying to hide something. Similarly, if a person speaks to you without taking their gaze away from you for long, they may be trying to threaten or intimidate you with their gaze. It is alright to look away periodically. However, shifting gaze constantly is a red flag.

- When you are addressing a group of people, closely observe the ones who are nodding excessively or in a more exaggerated manner. These are the people who are most concerned about your approval. They are anxious about making a positive impression and want to be in your "good books."

- People who are nervous or anxious tend to fidget with their hands or objects. Other signs of nervousness also include excessive blinking, tapping feet, and constantly running one's hand over the face.

- When an entire group walks into the room, how do you analyze who the leader or decision maker is? Quickly observe everyone's posture. The leader will most likely walk with a straight posture, with shoulders pulled out. Subconsciously, they are trying to occupy maximum space to convey authority over their team. Standing straight and pulling back shoulders increases a person's physical frame. It makes them come across as much bigger than they actually are. This is why people in power love to keep this posture to show their influence over a group or place.

- Expressions are the windows into a person's emotional state. When a person is amazed or surprised, their eyebrows are raised, and the upper eyelids widen. Similarly, the mouth gapes open. Expressions can often overlap, so watch for microexpressions that can reveal precise emotions.

- For instance, raised eyebrows can also reveal fear. Look for other micro expression clues to determine the exact emotion. If a person is experiencing fear, the eyebrows will be raised and pulled together with tensed lower eyelids, while the two corners of their lips will appear stretched. Similarly, a person's surprise is expressed by eyebrows pulled up and a lowered jaw. Learn to read the entire face, especially microexpressions, if you want to learn more about how a person is feeling.

- Since microexpressions occur in fractions of seconds, they are virtually impossible to fake. For instance, notice how when people are being deceptive, their mouths will slightly angle differently. Similarly, their eye movements become more rapid, the nostrils flare a little bit, and they purse their lips together (a subconscious gesture signaling their lips are sealed, or they won't reveal the truth). Since these split expressions are driven by the subconscious, this makes them involuntary, and it is almost impossible to manipulate them.

- Enlarged pupils reveal intense emotions such as excitement, elation, delight, surprise, and interest. When a person is attracted to you or truly delighted to see you, their pupils will involuntarily enlarge.

- The direction of a person's feet can also determine what's going on in their mind. Since feet aren't the first thing on anyone's mind, it's harder to manipulate body language related to legs and feet. If a person's feet are pointing away from you, they are subconsciously signaling their need to escape. However, if their feet are pointed toward you, they are interested or in agreement with what you are saying.

- Typical signs of frustration and stress are clenched jaws, wrinkled eyebrows, and tensed neck. The person's words notwithstanding, if you observe any of these signs, he or she may be undergoing a stressful situation that they are trying to conceal. The trick for reading people's emotions accurately is to keep an eye out for a clear mismatch between verbal and nonverbal clues.

- Observe a person's walk to tune in to their feelings. People with a heavier gait along with low gravity while moving their legs are most likely hurt, stressed, frustrated, or depressed. People who walk with a slower and more relaxed pace are reflecting upon something. Notice how confident, happy, and goal-oriented people walk swiftly in one direction.

- Observing a person's eye movements is a near accurate way of gauging how they are feeling since our eye movements are connected to precise brain functions. Our eye movements have an established pattern depending on the brain function or type of information we are trying to access. For instance, if an individual is caught in an internal conflict or dilemma (to either speak the truth or lie), there is a likelihood that they will tend to look towards their left collarbone. Darting sideways from one side to another can be a red flag that indicates deception.

- Proxemics is a subtopic within body language that talks about how people reveal their feelings and emotions through the physical distance they maintain with other people during the process of face-to-face interaction or communication. It is a very useful nonverbal signal for understanding a person's thought process or state of mind.

Psychologists and body language experts believe that the amount of physical distance we maintain while interacting with a person helps establish the dynamics of our relationship with them or reveals our emotions about them.

A person who isn't standing very close to you may not be emotionally open or receptive to you. They may have a tendency to closely guard their emotions or give only a little of themselves to the interaction. Such people may be more emotionally guarded and closed. You may need to make extra effort to get them to drop their guard and feel less intimidated. It may be a defense mechanism against being emotionally hurt or vulnerable.

On the other hand, if a person is leaning in your direction, they may subconsciously convey being emotionally open, or they trust you with their feelings. They may also be more interested in what you are speaking about.

Tone

The tone, volume, pitch, and emphasis of a person's voice can help you decode the hints that can help you tell what they are feeling. For example, if you notice plenty of inconsistencies in the tone of their voice as they speak, they are probably very angry, hurt, excited, or nervous. Ever notice how your voice shakes when you speak in a rage or are nervous about something? It can also be a sign the person is lying.

Similarly, if a person is speaking louder or softer than their regular volume, something may be amiss. Again, a person's tone is a dead giveaway. Sometimes people say something that sounds like a compliment. However, upon examining their tone closely, you realize the sarcasm and the condescension with which it was uttered.

The tone in which an individual ends their sentence says a lot about what they are trying to convey even with similar verbal clues. For example, if a person completes their sentence on a raised note, they are doubtful of something or are asking a question. Similarly, if they finish the sentence with a flat tone, they are pronouncing a statement or judgment. Watch out for how people end their sentences to get a clue about their inner feelings.

Again, the words people emphasize can help you uncover their true feelings. For instance, if an individual gets to say, "Have you borrowed the blazer?" while emphasizing "borrowed," it indicates their doubt over whether you have borrowed, stolen, or done something else to the blazer. However, if the emphasis is on "you," they aren't sure if it is you or someone else who has borrowed the blazer.

I also like to look at pauses between phrases to know about the person's attitude, emotions, and intentions. For example, if a person pauses after saying something, it could be because what they just said is extremely important to them, or they truly believe in it. Sometimes, a person pauses to seek validation or feedback from others. The speaker wants to gauge your reaction to what they said since it is important for them.

When people are in a more emotionally unstable or negative frame of mind (angry, hurt, or upset), their voice tends to be higher pitched or squeaky. They are most likely losing a grip on their emotions or aren't able to regulate their emotions effectively. Notice how, when people are very angry, their voice becomes more screechy and squeaky, as if they are about to cry.

The Speed of a Speech

A person's emotions clearly impact the speed of their speech. Notice how you start talking much faster than your normal rate of speech, or words per minute, when you are angry or upset. A rapid speech can convey lack of organization, uncertainty, or lack of clarity. The person is not very comfortable with speaking and is just trying to finish throwing their words. Again, a slower than usual pace translates into low self-confidence, inability to express emotions, inability to come to terms with one's emotions, lack of emotional reassurance, and other similar feelings.

Verbal Clues

A person's choice of words can say a lot about what they are thinking and feeling. Words are symbolic of our thoughts and feelings which, when combined with nonverbal clues, give us a comprehensive understanding of their emotional state.

The brain we have as humans is a miracle that one cannot unravel. When we think, or process rational and logical thoughts, we tend to use nouns and verbs. Conversely, when we attempt to express our thoughts or feelings in a verbal or written format, there is a tendency to use more adverbs and adjectives.

Any basic sentence features a subject and a verb. For example, "I walked." When a person adds more words to it, they can indicate their feelings or personality. For example, "I walked fast," can indicate a sense of urgency, fear, or insecurity. There are clear reasons why people use specific words over others.

Similarly, there is a hidden meaning behind what people say. Through their choice of words, people reveal emotions left unsaid.

Let's say you booked a table to take your family out for dinner at one of the fanciest, fine dining restaurants that recently opened in your neighborhood. The server greets you courteously and directs you to your table. What follows is an amazing dining experience.

The waiter introduces each of the seven courses in an informative yet engaging style, while you dine and enjoy wine in an upscale ambiance. After you enjoy a hearty meal and call for the tab, the waiter inquires if you enjoyed the food. You reply with, "The entrées were good."

The waiter doesn't look very delighted, even if what you said is a compliment in your opinion. Those four words you uttered reveal your real opinion about the food. It implies that other than the entrées, everything else was pretty average or the only thing that stood out during the entire meal were the entrées.

Did you actually say everything else other than the entrées was average? No. Then why did the waiter look crestfallen at your statement? It true that many individuals pass a lot of information through what they said and unsaid things. Gather the hidden meaning or subtext behind what people say to tune in to their inner feelings. Notice how sometimes people will say, "You look very lovely today." It can either mean you look plain every day (which is a more passive-aggressive kind of statement), or you are looking exceptionally good today compared to other days.

Another powerful clue about what people are thinking or feeling is noticing how they talk about other people. A number of researchers discovered that merely asking participants to rate positive and negative traits of three other people revealed a lot about the participants' social competence, general well-being, other people's perception of them, and their mental health.

It was observed that an individual's inclination to view other people in a positive manner was a strong indication of their own positive emotions. There is a strong link between seeing others in a more positive light and being emotionally stable, happy, productive, and enthusiastic.

On the other hand, viewing others in a negative light bears a strong correlation with a general sense of dissatisfaction, low self-esteem, anti-social behavior, and narcissism. People who hold plenty of negative emotions tend to perceive other people in a poorer or more negative light. This can also be an indication of emotional issues, mental health conditions, or a personality disorder. Again, emotions aren't good or bad but are reflections of how you are feeling. If a person experiences more negative emotions for others around them, it can be a clue to how they really feel about themselves.

If a person says that they "made up their mind" after plenty of deliberation, the phrase indicates a mindset that is high on logic and rational thinking. The individual may be more contemplative and practical by nature. They may examine all the options available before arriving at a particular decision. These are not your likely contenders for a snap of the moment decisions.

Do you know what metalanguage is? It is the intended words behind the words you speak. You don't say something directly but reveal it through the words you use. For example, notice how when people want to get someone to agree with what they've said, they'll always place yes, done, or okay followed by a question mark at the end. For example, "I can't hand in the project today. I'll submit it tomorrow, okay?" It is like manipulating the other person to agree.

To further increase your social-emotional quotient, pay attention to the sounds people utter, other than coherent words. Moaning, grunting, sighing, and so on, can reveal a lot. Sometimes, these sounds will complement the words the speaker is using to make the message even more persuasive. However, at other times, there may be a mismatch between the person's words and sounds.

For example, someone may say, "I am having a really good day," followed by a sigh, which can indicate they are simply being sarcastic and are in fact having a bad day. You can even understand more about what a person really means when you observe their words and other miscellaneous sounds they make.

Environmental Clues

A person's immediate environment says a lot about their emotional state. For instance, a messy, unclean, or disorganized space can indicate a lack of clarity of emotions or thoughts. Of course, everything has to be analyzed within a context. Someone may have an unkempt house because they are too busy to tidy it up and doesn't have housekeeping help.

All of us have certain spaces around us that are inaccessible that we don't really bother cleaning or organizing (space behind the cupboard or under the bed). These are spaces that we wouldn't normally clean. If such spaces are immaculately clean or organized, it can indicate anxiety or a disorder (obsessive-compulsive disorder).

Well-organized and clean spaces can indicate clarity of emotions or control over one's emotions. The person tends to be more reflective and introverted by nature. Similarly, people who are outwardly focused, or extroverts, tend to be surrounded by chaos.

This isn't pop psychology, but it is based on clear principles of how the environment around us is created through our actions, which themselves are directed by our subconscious thoughts and emotions. For example, using bright, vibrant, and bold prints in your décor or attire can be a sign of confidence, emotional self-assurance, and independence of thought or opinion. Likewise, a home with brighter and more vibrant colors is an indication of being bold, emotionally expressive, and outgoing. These people are not afraid of taking risks and are more than capable of understanding the needs and feelings of other people. More subtle colors imply inward directed emotions, or an introverted personality. These people may not be too receptive to another person's feelings and emotions.

People who hold on to old objects or hoard various objects can be excessively emotional, sensitive, or sentimental. They find it tough to move away from their past emotions or are still ridden by feelings of shame, regret, and guilt related to the past. These are people who latch on to old memories and can't release the emotions that hold them back.

When you use these verbal and nonverbal principles to understand people, your social-emotional quotient invariably increases.

Chapter 7: Emotional Intelligence and Relationships

Our relationships are our support system. A vital road to success is being able to recognize harmful relationships and discarding them accordingly. Also, you must be able to categorize your relationships and know which ones build you up the most.

Do you wish that your relationship was better or closer? If so, you don't need to visit a therapist for couples. Instead, you can improve your relations by applying emotional intelligence to the mix. We've gone over what the term means: using your feelings and moods to effectively live your life and have a positive impact. There are exercises as outlined in this book that will help you manage your emotions and gain the skills needed to help you interact with other people in a better way.

How can EQ Improve your Relationship?

No matter what problem you are facing in your relationship, you can improve it. As we've already mentioned in previous chapters, people with high emotional intelligence enjoy success in more areas than people who don't, and close relationships are no exception to this. Think about it this way: does anyone ever think about leaving their marriage because they have a partner who is too attentive, too understanding, or too encouraging and supportive? Once you apply EQ to the relationship you have with your partner, you can miraculously transform it. But where should you begin?

Building up Awareness in your Relationship

A high awareness of self will let you know what emotional factors you need in order to thrive and be happy. For a relationship to thrive and be happy, however, you and your significant other need to become aware of which emotional factors are needed so you can help each other meet your needs. The reason why people get into relationships in the first place is because these factors were being met when the relationship began.

Necessary Emotional Factors and How to Find Them

But the factors we need to thrive and grow are always changing, meaning that having EQ here refers to staying aware of those factors and whether they are being met on both sides. As soon as partners can sense that their relationship is helping them to grow into a better person, they will want to continue it. Here are the steps to doing this:

- **Make a List of the Emotional Factors you Need**: Here you will write down the top three emotional factors needed for you to feel fulfilled in a relationship. Have your partner do the same.

- **Make a List of the Factors you think They Need:** Now you will write down what you believe are the top three emotional factors needed by your partner in order to feel fulfilled. Have them also make a list for you.

- **Trade Lists:** Now you will trade lists and each read them and have a discussion afterward. This is a good way to generate fresh ideas to meet the required emotional factors for each of you.

Identifying and Managing Emotions in your Relationship

Important results from research on emotions has proven that they play a direct role in how well (or poorly) people perform. Certain feelings like anxiety or anger can nourish or stand in the way of relationships, while feelings such as optimism, enthusiasm, and confidence have a tendency to make them more productive. One emotion that nearly always gets in the way and has long-term negative effects is depression. What this implies is that relationships able to handle anxiety or anger in a positive way and that stay away from depression and nurture optimism, enthusiasm, and confidence will become healthier and more rewarding.

Why You Should Know about Contagious Emotions

Managing feelings in a relationship is difficult. It's the landscape that happens as a result of you and your partner's feelings that involves the contagion of emotions. This refers to the fact that feelings are similar to a virus in how they can spread between people. You can actually catch the anxiety, depression, or anger of your partner, or you can infect your loved one with your own enthusiasm and confidence.

How to Use this Phenomenon to your Advantage

In order to use this phenomenon to benefit your relationship, you have to know how to manage the feelings that are influencing your relations. Here are some skills you can work on for this.

- **Learn how to Relax at Will:** If you can make yourself relax at will, it shows that you know how to regulate your feelings. This will let you become immunized against negative emotions from your partner, letting you keep perspective, which has a tendency to get lost when both partners are in a bad state of mind. Negative feelings like depression or anxiety will heighten your feeling arousal and lead to a rigidity in your mental state, making it harder to act productively and accurately interpret what is happening. This can lead to a loud argument or one of you storming away.

- **The Benefit of Regulating your Emotions:** But when both of you learn how to regulate these feelings, you can stay rational and calm, making accurate assessments of what is happening and freeing yourself from the negative impact of another's feelings. You don't need to shout back when your partner shouts at you or catch their anxiety when they are fretting about bills. You should stay calm in such emotions to foster your relationship to a better zone amid any challenges.

- **Practice Exercises for Relaxation Together:** Every day for the following eight weeks, start practicing exercises for relaxation with your loved one. You will find that this helps both of you manage your feelings instead of letting them drive you apart.

These tips, along with the key points in the last chapter, will help you guide your relationship to a better place. Building awareness in your relationship and working against catching emotions like fear, anxiety, or anger from each other is a great first step to take.

Chapter 8: Creative Summary of Building Self-Confidence

Emotionally intelligent people are self-confident in nature. They have confronted their innermost demons and have emerged victorious. It is essential to be self-confident in order to be emotionally intelligent. In this chapter, we will discuss how we can become more confident of ourselves through four easy methods.

Identify Your Weaknesses

The first step in the journey of becoming self-confident is becoming aware of the self. The foremost task for anyone who wants to become self-confident is to identify their weaknesses. These are areas of your life that make you unsure of yourself. It can be your personality trait or a physical trait. Always remember there is no such weakness that one cannot overcome. All it takes is hard work and dedication. Most people do not correctly identify their weakness and the areas that make them feel insecure of themselves and, as a result, suffer from a demotivated attitude in their lives. Becoming self-confident helps one make better decisions in life and achieve success without any ado. It is essential that you familiarize yourself with your shortcomings. It is

71

no good living in denial or with an escapist attitude. You can run from your demons but cannot break free until you confront them head-on.

Plan Out Your Course of Action

Having once identified your problem areas, chalk out a course of action upon which you will act. Set aside a fixed amount of time from your daily schedule where you will single-mindedly address your concerns. If it is losing weight then you will exercise for that period of time not concerning yourself with other mortal affairs of this life. Unless such dedication is shown, change remains a distant dream for most of us. Do not set very lofty targets for they demotivate you from the very start. Set yourself realistic and manageable targets that you can foresee yourself achieving in a relatively short time span. Most people do not even initiate this change required to gain self-confidence.

Act Upon It

Having once identified your weaknesses, it becomes the time to act upon them. You must not be hesitant of a lifestyle change or a mental makeover because once you decide to overcome your weaknesses, your life will change for certain. Most people remain snugly wrapped up in the cocoon of their comfort zones and don't want to step out and sweat it out. It is essential to remember that you will have to endure much in order to change the way you are. It won't come to you while you are relaxing on your couch. Be it losing fat or gaining muscle, be it succeeding in an examination or in a real-life relationship, unless you work toward it, you will achieve nothing. Hence, do not hesitate to act once having familiarized yourself with your shortcomings.

Reward Yourself

Rewards are an imperative to work harder and with more dedication. Unless you reward yourself along with your journey of transformation, the journey will appear too arduous to complete. Rewards in no way mean stepping out of the line and deviating yourself from your goal but just a little token of pampering. This little reward gives you further motivation and keeps you going. This is to show that you love yourself and appreciate all the efforts that you are making in order to induce a lifestyle change.

Conclusion

There is a wide variety of people in our modern society. Some are high achievers, others are moderate achievers or average people. What is the determining factor making the individuals to be different? What is the factor for fulfillment? More and more people are coming to realize that there is something which differentiates people and that most of it can be developed. More and more people are keying into their emotional intelligence and their positive intelligence to achieve fulfillment. We have highlighted these important concepts in this book and we know that a careful practice of the principles embedded in this book will result in mind-boggling achievement. We hope you experience it in your life.

Emotional intelligence gives you the capacity to tackle a number of challenging circumstances. You will also find that as you meditate on a daily basis, your intuition will truly become honed. There is a very good reason to want to do this as well. Over the course of your life, you have been programmed by everything that happened in your life. If you watch TV, you get programmed into believing that certain products add to your lifestyle. If you watch too much TV of a mindless nature, you tend to become mindless and this exercise once a day will help you to come back into the real world and find the reality of life is actually much simpler than you may imagine.

I wish you well in your journey and would suggest you read the book several times and implement the suggestions made within its pages to improve your levels of emotional intelligence and start to life a life full of joy and fulfilment.